In a Rich Country

In a Rich Country

poems
Edward Wilson

GRAYSON BOOKS
West Hartford, CT
www.GraysonBooks.com

ISBN: 978-0-9994327-8-5
Library of Congress Control Number: 2019932544

interior and cover designs by Cindy Mercier
cover artwork by Edward Rice

for
Elizabeth Duncan Wilson
1909-1975

Acknowlededgments

My thanks to the following journals in which these poems first appeared.

The American Poetry Review: "August."

The Georgia Review: "Balloon Man," "Camellias in Snow," "East Tennessee," "Farmers, Muhlenberg County, Kentucky—What They Didn't Say," "I'm a Guest at the Wedding of Horowitz's," "Lakehurst," "Oyster," "Rock," "Sunset," "Willadean MacIllvane."

The Midwest Quarterly: "Fighter Pilot."

Poetry: "That Weekend Our Team Won."

The South Carolina Review: "The Miner."

The Southern Poetry Anthology, Volume 5: Georgia: "Boy," "Smoke knows."

The Southern Poetry Review: "For the Woman Weeping at a Red Light," "Moonrise," "Santa Fe," "Thriller Writer."

Town Creek Poetry: "At Moot Point," "Ben Ross," "In Blue," "There is a River under the Lake."

I am indebted to the National Endowment for the Arts for support and a fellowship which helped bring these poems to publication.

Contents

III

I

For the Woman Weeping at a Red Light

It's like watching the dead
winter yard through a window above
the radiator, the glass itself
rippling almost. Or this street
the August sun has slapped
hour after hour until parking meters
are a line of woozy drunks
and even the brick stores billow
like sheets on the line.

You have been carrying it all day,
a glass impossibly full,
and didn't know until this wavering
of everything spilled over.

And not because you are unhappy.
You've lived long enough to know
that love comes home exhausted
and falls asleep on the couch
with his shoes on.

The tune on the radio, the limping boy—
whatever's jogged your elbow
isn't dramatic, unbearable. It's
hardly even yours yet, though if
you thrashed among the leaves like towhees
in the woodlot there would be something
in that sweet rot to seize on.

Meantime, there is no shame
in crying while the light is red.
You live in a rich country.
You have tears to spend.

Boy

He can hardly walk
but grinning up at us
he's steady on legs
plump as drumsticks.
The first sentence, first
shoelace tied, the first
note he'll learn to whistle
are for the future, over
the horizon. Just now
he's examining the
sidewalk, beads of
ants like a broken neck-
lace spilling away into
the grass. His mother
has yet to cry for his
first haircut. Just now
those strands lift in the
breeze and the sun
ignites them. Like soft
electricity. Articulate as
spider silk, telling us
what he's thinking, who
he is, when all we have
are words.

Ben Ross

That day at Gathiel Simpson's farm
we followed Ben Ross down the path
to a gray rock face he struck with his pick
and bent to see clams in his hand
smaller than my little finger's nail.

        From limestone. Mississippian.
300 million years.

        The world changed
suddenly. The ground I stood on
was a myth, a story—older,
unimaginably—yet made of days, like
this one, the sun moved slowly over.

        And walking back,
he stopped and said, "Do you smell that?"

Melons. Warm and sweet. Easing
into the weeds, me just behind, he pointed
to the tangled nest of copperheads.
Deadly and calm.   At home.   At ease.

The Miner

He gripped the banister and plodded up the stairs
like a narrow-gauge engine on a grade.
I hardly noticed and pushed past with a jar
of fresh pond water to label and drip on a slide

in my make-shift lab, the unused office
off the waiting room. But I forgot the microscope
and listened when he sat with his back to the rippled glass
door, counting his breath like change in a sock.

And I followed when he shuffled after the nurse.
Under the shirt, he was as white as her uniform
except for a blue-black mark—no bruise,
but the tattoo a lump of coal stamped on his arm.

My father joked but their eyes swung far
apart when his stethoscope touched ribs. Listening hard
my father watched something under the floor.
The miner looked out the window and examined clouds.

Willadean Macillvane

One way back from downtown Saturday
afternoon was through Freddie's father's
lumberyard while the blaze erased the
double feature, a serial, cartoons—half
a day in the Palace's magical dark.
There were piles of logs, a cone of saw-
dust higher than a house—sand-smooth
and pale outside, but wet and steamy
if you scooped a hole out with your hand.
Big as a poker table, studded with teeth,
asleep now in its shed, the saw we heard
week-days from the open classroom
windows squalling through barked logs.
Sneaking by, I could confuse myself
threading the maze of ricks of rough green
planks stacked twice my height, toward
home beyond the barely creek in its hardly
ditch that dribbled through the canebrake
past Willadean's—a streetless house, if
you didn't count the path through weed,
heedless of paint, committed to falling
down.
        She was the poorest of the clutch
of us that teachers brooded over and bore
annually from grade to grade, but with
the best of names dactyling over the tongue
like water over the stones of a highland
brook.
        Most days of the year for more
than ten, we sat at desks in the same
room sharpening pencils, outgrowing
shoes. I must have held her hand in
one child-chain or another we were
commanded to assemble when there
were streets to cross. No one I knew was
her friend. We couldn't have swapped
a dozen words. And when I left, I didn't
say goodbye. Still, it's her face of the
bushel I remember that comes most often,
and unbidden. Not for its beauty, but for
the way it has arranged itself, composed

and facing now, as it did then, patiently,
for no good reason, whatever it meets,
the next thing coming, as if it were a gift.

When My Friend

the magician showed up,
drinks appeared from thin
air. Bills, unfolding, flew to
barmaids. No coin would stay
in a pocket or under the cup
where I knew it had to be.
They'd flash from ears and
noses, tumble across his
knuckles. In his hands the deck
unfurled like a peacock's tail.
Cards riffled in arcs from palm
to palm. The one I'd picked
and slipped back in the pack,
hopped from the bartender's
pocket. And he would laugh
through his bushy mustache
to see my face—slack-jawed,
amazed—Thomas' gullible
brother—hungry for miracles.

Roadblock

was his nickname, and come
by honestly, when he was
county sheriff. Diminished,
now, by at least 100 pounds,
under a quilt that stretches
from his chin over his toes,
he fills the Barcalounger like
a model of the southern
Appalachians—gentle bulges,
dips, and folds.

He was a repo man—east,
in Harlan county, along
the West Virginia line, where
4th grade kids stuck pistols
in their belts to go to school,
where, before his clients
gave them up, they'd torch
their trucks, shove them off
an edge laughing as
they pin-wheeled down
into the creek.

We watch a costume drama
on the muted screen across
the room—Yul Brenner as
the pirate Jean Lafite, Heston
as General Jackson, charged
with defending New Orleans.
As we're remembering things—
how they have or haven't
changed, who knew who, back
when, who's kin to whom—we
glance up to see if they
can work their problems
out and beat the Brits.

Now, he runs political campaigns—
local and state, got the governor
re-elected. He knows what's
what, who's who. His other
businesses surround the house
like planets orbiting a star.
A collection agency. A garage—
a big one—heavy machinery and
furniture. Two more devoted
to antiques—which before we
leave his wife will take us through.

(And in them, so much glass.
Hutches, sideboards, tables,
boxes under tables, freighted
with it, depression to bone china,
jelly glass to demitasse)

Here, on the dining table
an epergne hefts fist-fulls
of millefiori. Old clocks march
through the quarter hours like
a squad of fuzzled codgers
drilling—almost in formation,
almost in time. On shelves
around the room, more lumps
of glass—beveled, incised,
heavy enough to club a man
to death. Others, web fragile.
Curves and whorls stolen from
orchids. Delicate as fresh ice
on a puddle. And more small
things that might be Sevres,
Meissen, Spode, Limoges.

And portraits that could be
merchant's children, planters' boys
and girls. Their cheeks still
blushing from the painter's brush.

The Brits are on the run.

Warrior

Last night in a Gallup bar he climbed down
into the earth-cool dark. Tribes

of names that danced in his head
rode away south, their black robes flapping.

His own staggered off past a cottonwood
and dried up. Weeds caught him.

The wind snuffs around this morning
but nothing disturbs his ceremonial quiet.

At the top of the ladder the sky waits
like the turquoise eye of the Anglo barmaid.

Thriller Writer

At the keyboard every day, new ideas,
fresh plots, hot sex, a kaleidoscope of clever
wholesale murder that villains with accents,
or whiz-bang techno- geeks I invent
endlessly contrive. Ex-KGB, ex-CIA,
Mossad, ancient Nazis, swarthy Arab
terrorists. Sociopaths driven to scheme
like OCD chess masters since when they cried,
their mothers failed to pick them up.

My own phones half a dozen times a day.
My wife won't answer when she sees the number.
"We're having a roast tonight," my mother says.
"Your father should be home by six."

My father has been dead 11 years, almost.
She has two rooms in a facility. They
bathe her, feed her, come when she'll touch
the button by her bed. I see her Sundays,
in a huge, bright room—one wall all glass.

The lawn beyond is manicured—raised and
sculpted beds, a fountain in the pool. Her hair
is done. There are dozens like us working at
a conversation through the afternoon.

On the hill beyond the garden, I imagine
a sniper. He has a mission. He is pitiless.
He's taken days to crawl to his position: perfect,
invisible, with an unobstructed field of fire.
Slowly, deeply, he takes another breath. His index
finger barely strokes the trigger. The cross-hairs
hover on her skull. And then on mine.

Henry

They pinned his hip when the porch step gave way
but he wouldn't get up. Here, they wheel
him out and park him in the solarium
Sundays when you visit. "Uncle Henry,"

you say, crouched in front of eyes noncommittal
as windows flat to the afternoon sun.
"It's Ed … I'm here … Remember me?"
But no one seems to be at home and your voice

wanders as if it had heels to crunch
the broken glass on the parlor floor. A thread
snaps and more batting erupts from the couch.
The wallpaper sags and adds another wrinkle.

In the thrilling dark of an upstairs closet
he hears and hugs his knees closer till
the Indians, the Pirates, the Cannibals pass by.
He knows if he doesn't giggle, he won't be caught.

Fighter Pilot

When that heart raging for kerosene
snaps its word like a bone, growls
its one long vowel over the hangars,

wings are an afterthought.
Pure hunger lifts me.

I punch it. The afterburner's
bloodshot eye scowls at the ground
and I am gone.

You, fearing for your crystal,
quivering with your windows,
will never track me—

even the thunder I drop
falls farther and farther behind.

Less than a name, my past bled dark
in the West, I would rumble here—

brain thin as gas, gone out among the God-
whirl, patterned fire of constellations—

but I drop to the stunned wink
of the runway, dim streaked tarmack,
where I flicker and flame out:

a spark, guttering, a cinder passed
from arms to arms—wife, lover, bartender.

Prophet

"Time," as my mother said, "is anklin' on."
Has ankled, indeed. No sackcloth and ash.
No locusts for appetizer, main course or
dessert. No kings to berate. Now the elect
are chastened on the Op-ed page while the
stiff-necked errant come to justice on Jerry
Springer and Dr. Phil. I wear a tie to work,
pay taxes, and, like you, worry about
good schools. Still, there is wilderness
enough in each of us to wander 40 days
and silence to entice that still, small voice.
When it whispers—like an old woman,
perhaps, a girl, or the man beside me on
the subway reading the morning paper—
I am compelled to speak. I tweet, as needed,
and post a weekly blog.

If asked, "What doest thou here?" I'd be hard
pressed and repeat, "I am no better than my
fathers who are dead." Indeed, you'd think
that after all these years eavesdropping on
the numinous some wisdom would accrue.
But that Presence has no talent for clarity
or narrative. It speaks in piths and gists.
Benighted as any, if not most, I'm left
with riddles by the mouthful to dispense.

The universe is huge and old, and rare
things happen all the time, but I'm no longer
all that curious. My fate, as Plato says
of each of us, is not that interesting. And
all I'm sure of seems to shrink—a few bright
pebbles in the palm. I know each morning
shaving for the mirror, the lines my face
has fallen into say it can't be long until
the fist of my heart won't climb the rope
of my blood. And it's unlikely I'll be
summoned back, like Samuel. I know the
price of admission here with light and air
and sky is nothing less than everything
and certain to be paid. And I know, too,

the monks and quantum physicists have got
it right. All that we're given—this only,
always-blooming moment—holds us in its
instant, face-to-face. If you have a question,
ask me. Read my lips.

Pete

He was never good with words
but he had a smile you wanted more of
and no tool was a stranger.

He built this house from the ground up.
The windows slide, the doors swing true
as when he hung them 40 years ago.

There's never been a crack in a wall
or the ceiling of the room where he sits
watching the program she's turned on.

Half his face is noncommittal.
One hand lies in his lap like yesterday's
fish washed up on a beach.

The other holds it,
fingers moving, searching
for something to fix.

Love and Death and Chickens

That racket—loud, distressed—
toddled me down the backyard slope,
will-less as a beach ball and

less accurate. The scorched washtub
propped up on bricks. Bea feeding kindling
to the fidgety orange underneath.

On the grass, an eye looked up
from its feathery head appraisingly,
detached.

Hens thrashing red and gold, like huge frantic
peonies at the ends of her arms,
my mother turned,

flung them away and caught me up to watch
that mad dance. Hardly enough yard
to hold it while it lasted.

Balloon Man

Not the jolly one
which if unmoored
would bounce and roll
through thickets of glee,
childrens' pointing fingers,
their mouths O's
of delight,

but the gaunt one
breakdancing in front of
acres of bargains
at the used car lot.

Bent at the middle,
collapsed, head in the gravel
then springing up again,
stubby arms miming alarm.

All day broken and spliced.
like a rabbi rocking
at the wall, like Sisyphus
without a boulder or a hill.

And it goes on after
the strings of lights are lit.
You'd think that whipsnap
jerk would set him free.
But something holds
his feet to the fan.

Even in the dark
these disconsolate calisthenics
buckle and leap
full of implacable air.

The Stars

fall down when you sit
in a chair on the patio
with the third drink
in your hand.

Your wife, the kids
eat in the kitchen with
nothing to say.

You used to know
the constellations by heart.
What came up, went down.

When. The seasons, nights,
meteors would most likely
scar the sky.

You'll come in
when the chill comes up,
when the vodka bottle
in the fridge is empty.

In bed, dreams wake
you in a sweat. No sense
to them but the taste of how
they make you feel.

What difference
between them
and the connect-the-dots
old shapes wheeling
above the house?

Those gods, creatures,
men the ancients watched,
made up stories about—

they're just stars.

Farmers, Muhlenberg County

What they didn't say

Not Goodbye. They can wait,
hunkered down, turning the plug
of dark fire between blunt thumbs
and the knife blade as if
30 years were a Saturday afternoon
while I remember the square
around them.

         And nothing about
what they'd learned four paces
behind a mule opening long furrows
in late winter grass like
old cloth torn slowly, turning
the earth gently as a nurse,
nudging it awake.

         Walking by
I had the look. I was going—
like the salesman to his brand
new Ford, the sample cases
in the backseat full.

         And words,
for them, take time to shoulder up
green through the dirt.

         After all,
they've welcomed back sons who sat
in loose uniforms looking past
the porch, the yard and through the hill
beyond like it was glass until
they left again.

The hardware
store is there to lean against.
They watch what History, across
Main Street beneath the courthouse
dome, might think of next.

They chew and spit.
And they keep off the grass.

II

Lakehurst

For most of us, buoyed up by dreams
like a million cubic feet of hydrogen,
it is May 6th, 1937.

When I say *Lakehurst* you
should recall the weightless silver
bulk of the Von Hindenburg just as it
flares and the skeletal girders cage
fire an instant before they warp
like the commentator's voice straining
against panic and disbelief.

But not yet. Not yet.

Drizzle
frays the overcast and we float
above the parquet of New Jersey, placid
as a waltz from the aluminum piano, while
the irony this poem depends on gathers
like static in the folds of the cashmere
scarf draped around your neck, my neck,
perfecting a spark.

Standing here
at the broad lounge window, watching
the drenched ground crew below jiggle
like puppets at the ends of the anchor lines,
we dismiss the tickle of electricity
that lifts our hair.

Glasses we raised
to the statue at the harbor mouth lifting
her torch are still in our hands as the
pylon eases for the nose and one of us asks:

What was the name of this place?

Lakehurst.

The Fountain of Youth

is in a trailer park
a few miles down the road
from Green Cove Springs.
Not there exactly, but just past
Edith's tarnished *Vagabond*
sagging on its tires
down the vague path
through palmetto scrub
almost to the lightning topped
loblolly where two osprey
nest for the river view up and
down the wide St. Johns.

It's nothing you'd imagine
drinking from. Hardly bigger
than a washtub. Tea colored,
infused with root and soil
under leaf and needle fall.
They've found a dram a week
works best for a proper mix of salt
and pepper in the hair, decorous
wrinkles, knees that bend,
an uncomplaining back.

If you find the chipped cup
on the nearby rock and dip it,
that sip might ignite
in every vein … and time
distend like railroad tracks
across Nevada leading away
forever from the nest of family,
thickets of friends.

Some would put it down
and turn back. Edith makes
marmalade out of windfall
oranges from the nearby
grove. Her neighbor, Roy,
searches out pine stumps,
splits them apart, sorts

the sticks and ties them
up for fatwood kindling.

At the stand by the road,
his bundles and her jars
spread out across the boards
with baskets of tomatoes,
melons, corn husk dolls,
sand dollars, loose shells,
shells glued on boards in
the shape of stars or
spelling a little shakily,
Welcome, Mother, Love.

If, while you browse,
touching this thing or that,
you introduce yourself,
they'll look up the way
you'd glance at midges,
squint past your shoulder
at the sunset like an angel's
flaming sword and pause
to recollect their names.

Talking Cure

My father was a drunk.
My mother too, in self-defense.
Their wars filled up the house
with noise and worse. Like gravel
in a hubcap. Blows to the walls
like limbs clubbing the roof
and no wind outside.

It wasn't meant for me,
but their aim was never good.

When he was alive and called
I hardly had a word to say—
spare change to a panhandler.
I've had to peel her face away
from the faces of the women
I've done my best to love.

They gave me enough to carry
to this quiet room. A wise one
said once, "Nothing's resolved,
only left behind."

To be cured is to be cleaned.
By water, smoke, by the Cherokees'
Black drink, since unlike Snake
in a tight spot, we can't wriggle through
or leave our skins behind
inside out like socks.

I have these words to work with
and a man I pay to listen.

Some days they burrow,
huddling, won't be roused.
Some days they leave my mouth
more like moths zigzagging
softly in his dim room, thrumming
the windows, or, surrendered,
folded on a lampshade.

Some days they fly
as if the ceiling and these walls
were less than mist. And where?
To St. Francis with his open arms
preaching in the garden?
To Ultima Thule?

Those specks in the sky
must be birds. Maybe glancing back.
Watching what I was. Seeing me
so far away. Behind. Below.
Watching them.

East Tennessee

Fields humped up
bordered with cedars.
Here and there a pale
flash of Cumberland
limestone like an ancient
creature rolling up.
Breaching. Never
far under the grass.

Few folk left now
with the bone so close
in their faces. Hard
to scrape a living
behind a mule. Hard
even to bury the dead.
People who if they
didn't shoot, fed you
and passed the jug.

Headlights hauling
the car from hollow
to hollow, turning
the dial—the little
stations still remember
and you can sing
along. Sometimes
whatever the fiddle
saws falls apart
and leaves a voice—

a wail like bare wire
lifting up and away
from the cedars along
the fencerows like dark
torches against a sky
the sun's forsaken into
which from somewhere
stars are wandering.

Cane Creek

As for this hollow, like a length
of lost rope, it curves through hills
with no aspiration to compete
with the mountains farther on. Flat
as a river bottom, about as wide
as the throw a kid with a decent
arm fielding a fly would make to
the catcher straddling home plate.
The two-lane blacktop road has no
patience with these twists and turns.
It has somewhere to go, straight
as it can. Not so the creek wandering
under it, away to the far slope
and back again the way a blind man
negotiates a hall--slowly, his out-
stretched fingers brushing first one
wall and then the other…
The few houses are well-kept,
freshly painted, yet no pick-ups on
the gravel drives, no one rocking
on the porch to watch the patch-
work fields across the road (none
larger than the limed rectangle
back in town where boys collide
on Friday nights) mostly gone
to weed: poke, Joe Pye, Queen Ann's
lace—sumac and alder where it's
wet. But there's a square of corn,
a week short of ripe and another
farther on. And farther still, where
the little tractor sits, a field for hay.
Alfalfa, cut—some laid in swales, some
rolled. Until, after more scrub and
weed, where the hollow begins
to end, the hillside slopes converge—
the way a bird at last light drops
to a pond, settles, and folds its
wings—off to the right, an old horse,
alone, at home in his pasture.

Santa Fe

All day the stream winds
down the mountain like
each of us taking the easy
way. A few cottonwoods
stand beside it as if it were
a parade—a small one,
trickling through town,
carrying a few leaves. Who
knows what the crows were
saying all afternoon in that
language like boys breaking
bottles at a dump? Now
the gnawed moon's fallen
west beyond Shiprock. In
the light from the open
door, a patch of snow beside
a bush where its shadow
curled and slept. And wood
smoke--all that's left of
childhood. And stars
coming out. So many, like
the forgotten, the lost,
turning through the night.
High. Far out of reach.

Moot Point

Pamlico River, Washington, N.C.

At dawn, mullet slap
the river. Here. There.
Hardly enough breeze
to wrinkle it awake.

Trees on the far shore—
the ragged hem of sky
(up before me and walking
away into forgetful blue).

Late last night at
the end of the dock, water
wide enough, gentle
enough to rock each star.

Now it offers up cloud.

A gull. A dog. A light
plane nattering the air-
port. A single halyard
strumming a mast.

I don't see anyone. Sun
starting to warm my back
like a father's hand.

The mountains are a good way
that way. The sea, this way.
Here, the river is wide
and slow and calm.

Burning Leaves

Only criminals do this now
given the ordinances.
Burning is left to the pros.
But tonight the blessed work
of miscreants is filling the sharp air
from grass blades to the first stars
with my childhood.

After a showy farewell
how easily the trees
let a whole life go—
over and done. All afternoon
we'd rake the piles and rows
then leap and roll in that soft crinkle
until our mothers called us in.

And what did my father think
down at the end of the yard
leaning on a rake with George
from next door—each
with a jelly glass of bourbon
and a common purpose—making ash
while orange as the seam
at the edge of the sky,
the flame was doing its work?

And when at last he closed
the kitchen door against the dark
he lifted me up against his sweater
cold as November air and
rich with the smoke of leaves.

Crabapples

On their own at the back
of the yard, away from the beds,
the loam and mulch, the rows
and stakes strung with twine
to give the viney ones
a leg up.

Small trees, a couple of them,
just right for small boys
learning the ancient primate
craft of climbing,

full of those tough nubbins
straining all summer,
still hardly marble-sized.

I wondered why she bothered
after weeks putting up tomatoes,
peppers, snap beans, bread
and butter pickles, corn

then onions and potatoes—
the ones that took no work
but digging up—hidden away
like feebleminded relatives
in the dim bins downstairs.

But one day the big pot
rocked and chuffed on the burner,
filled and refilled with water,
pectin, sugar, fruit, then strained
and sealed in jars.

And all afternoon, random
percussions from the pantry
as lids puckered and cooled.

Over the months , those shelves
unburdened themselves—
some jars wrapped in tissue paper
some handed over at a door

until, up this street, down another,
they, mostly, were dispersed.

It was a while before
I understood. Winter. Breakfast.
Light from the window. The jar
like a jewel spreading red
on the white tablecloth.

All the slow summer in my mouth.
The year again in every bite.

Night Clouds

Too much starlight
can take us away,
make us forget
what holds us here.

Those ancient patterns
whispering—as we might if
we sat at the end of the dock
at sunset and sang to midges
our oldest, deepest dreams.

But shapes not star or night sky
interpose—softest interruptions
of that snow drift susurration
on our shingles.

And while they pass, we come
to ourselves again—dry the dish,
turn down the sheets.

Shedding the glow of town,
they depart for fields and
where hills rise, drag
their bellies in pines
translating what they've heard
haphazardly—phrases
of rain, tattering the air.

Over and over, as best it can,
the grass tells the part it's heard.

And the river is diligent,
keeping to its errand,
murmuring on with its cargo
of toomuchforustoknow.

First Time

I didn't know
the last house was
the bootlegger's.
But George did.

Where we got the money
I don't know
wadded in our pockets
like notes from girls
we were embarrassed by
and glad to get.

But it was clear how
we'd be spending it.

He smoothed the bills,
passed the two half pints.

The glass was cool
and fit my hand.
The cork squeaked
when I twisted it.

Brown and burning,
it went down
like it knew the way.

It made me say
some things I didn't know
I could. It made me lie,
and want to.

It made me kneel down
on the blessed grass
and give it back.

That Weekend Our Team Won

There was a double feature at the drive-in,
a sock-hop in the gym. But somewhere
between church and youth fellowship,
sometime during that long coast down hill
Sunday afternoon, you went on
or got off forever.

A few of us even waved as you drove
away from the Dairy Queen. We knew the bend
that slung your father's car off the road
and the tree that caught it. We heard
how the radio still played
when the farmer came along.

The whole class went to your funeral.
We closed ranks in algebra and French
and got used to the idea while
the wreck rusted in the junkyard.
In June, you had your eulogy
 and a page of the annual to yourself.

Some nights when the house is quiet
We take it down and turn back.
That ring, still fuzzy with yarn,
hangs from your neck and you smile
at us trying to remember which movie,
what song, how much we won. You smile
as if you can't believe how it's turned out.

Since There Is No Time

I stroll past her roses—head-high,
nodding, fat as cabbages—and
climb the back steps to my tee-totaling,
Baptist, grandmother's kitchen who
gives me a geisha's smile as warm
as a cup of sake and a towel and
I blink back tears from fumes of vinegar
since she's making relish (the pot
immense enough to feed the Green Bay
Packers) and putting up the lot—
small arms fire in the pantry, the tops
of jars puckering as they cool.

And suddenly, since there is no time,
the pot is gone, the room's a bustle
with aunts, daughters, sisters-in-law
who ferry from the cornucopian stove
biscuits, corn-bread, assorted casseroles,
roasts in nests of new potatoes, hams
ringed with pineapple, pinned with cloves,
platters of birds shellacked with juice
out to the table where my grandfather
sits lean as he was with Pershing
in France.

        (and since there is no time,
out front, his first wife, the socialite,
steps from her Packard to the curb
wreathed in smiles and fur)

Gone the fixed Old Testament frown
that flushed his sons away like coveys
of quail. My uncles back at table now,
cousins mitosing, my father less the limp
on two good legs, the lost one
as it was before the double-barrel
coughed birdshot into his ankle, before,
before, he blocked the plate, ball in
his mitt as the runner rounding third,
slid home and snapped it just below the knee.

        (his first wife, too, across the room
with her one blue and her one green eye,
holding a devilled egg).
Since there is no time, the god
assigned to deal riffles the deck of all
our days and turns, for each of us, this
one, the best, face up on green baize.

Since there is no time, my mother
who taught Merle Travis in a one-room
schoolhouse, built fighters in the war,
ran a Pepsi bottling plant, plays piano
in the living room—a boogie-woogie
with a walking bass—her beau,
up from Lake Charles, standing behind,
his roadster pinging, cooling in the drive.

Since there is no time and this
banquet calls so many, the house
begins to fill with neighbors, friends,
the lost, forgotten, overlooked, those
who have wandered away, So many
they begin to rise and float like Chagall's
dream through every room and out
the open windows into a sky as blue
as it will ever be where the sun
dawdles as it did for Joshua before
Jericho and clouds, whiter than you
can remember, appearing like your breath
on the winter's coldest day, like mountains
taken with a notion to be wandering,
dimming the countryside a moment
as they pass like the shadow of a hand,
slowing like ocean liners, since there
is no time, coasting to a stop, mooring—
finally—to their piers of air.

I'm a Guest at the Wedding of Horowitz's

fingers and Chopin's brain. You used
to have to dress for such occasions. After dinner,
the carriage ride to claim your velvet plush
at the Weiner Musikverein. The light in the hall—

garnet, amber—echoing on cut stones
at fingers wrists necks, slithering over
bodices and sleeves. Back then, I would have been
too poor and tired from unloading freight at the dock
along the river, hacking apart a side of beef,
squinting over columns of figures at a desk.

It's dark in the room where I listen now,
on a pillow and good sheets, while the ceremony
proceeds. It is a strenuous union—
violent and glittering. I am not sentimental
about such performances, but

I am a devotee—drawn to these events
like an autograph hunter or a votary—at the opening
pressing the velvet rope, crowding the red carpet,
holding my phone above the beefy guys
they hire for security.

But, the nuptials—astonishing how these two dance
once they've pledged all to each other. The thrilled air
shivers to carry such a pas de deux. It lifts
and I lift—flying as I did so many times when
I was a child sleeping, dreaming I was flying.

Spring Song

I don't know what
made these hills lie
down.
       Maybe Ocean.
It was here once.
Maybe its old song
put them to sleep.

River finds a way
through, goes off
in that direction.

Light falls—flung
from its old catastrophe.
Once again change
is remembering green.

You've seen this before.
Convincing, almost.
Old song, almost new.

Whatever you might think
about it, Earth
still wants you, waits
for your next step.

You can feel it under
the floor, under
the soles of your shoes.

If you lie down, stretch
out, it will hold
you. Imagine wanting
so steadily. So long.

Severn

There were voices in the trees.

Severn no one said, but I understood.
Yet like no waking river, winding
toward the always calling sea.

And in no hurry. Glittering where
it meandered through low hills
in this valley contrived of peace
and light and green.

No one I knew, had lost, came walking
on the grass—changed or the same.
No kind, fair shape transmuted to
a horror. In that place, the worst
that happened was to wake.

The cottage close by where I stood
sparkled like flaked mica. Wattle and daub—
a ladder propped against the thatch.

There were orchards all around—
old apples, the limbs at once a froth
of blossom and bent with fruit.

And though I saw no one, there were
voices in the leaves that hardly moved
and children sang.

Had I listened harder,
had I stayed a little longer,
I could have told you
what they sang.

III

Smoke Knows

after so long locked
in a stick. It's just
using the fire.
It leaves us
a little whisper.
So we'll remember.
So when the time comes,
we'll know how.

In Blue

November
two hawks patrol
the river tracing
so slow spirals as
it goes wherever down
is steadily hauling
over the rocks
its load of glitter
and sun   that
philanthropist from
his high counting
house   filling our
pockets with
now   one coin
at a time.

August

is a girl in a print dress sweeping the porch.
Between strokes, she rests her chin on the handle of the broom.
She is waiting for the man who will give her griefs
like children and help her flesh sag.
His arms are dark and tough as mesquite,
but under the dust and buttons she knows his skin is pale.
When the crown of his hat punctures the horizon
she will have time to wash her face and bunch her hair in the mirror
before he rides close and stands at the well.
She will not answer at first but stand in the hallway dark
and watch him through the screen door
the bent tin dipper in his hand the white horse at his back
nuzzling the grass like a cold wind.

Sunflowers

They won't look the sun they yearn for in the eye
but they feel his gaze.

At the edge of the garden swelling for him
their huge heads hang, ashamed of their lank stalks.

Each day he passes them over.
They stare at the dirt and weep bees.

Rock

You thought you were
the stream, but you're
a rock. Another notion
the years proved wrong.

You've seen a lot go by.
Whatever points you made
aren't so sharp anymore.

But water, that gentlest
of didacts, let's you draw
your own conclusions. What

ever's happening's hurrying
along. And for the moment,
you're in the middle of it.
The ripples say it's so.

Kite

A kite is frightened
all the time.

It only wants to escape
and the sky seems
like the best idea.

All skin and bone
with yearning, a small boy
is its torturer.

Every tug of his hand
a glimpse
of the horizon
through bars.

It is like a stupid fish
that will never understand
it's hooked.

Clouds look down
on this struggle
like tourists from the windows
of a bus.

That dance—the wheeling
and darting—is
a prayer for the string
to break.

Camellias in Snow

Overnight, a topiarist
obsessed with white
has made an exhibition
of the neighborhood.

Enchanting as it is
after a while the eye,
(a hound unleashed),
casts about for color.

Hope is like this—alert
for any blessing peeking
through circumstance.

Seek and ye shall...
in this case a bush,
not burning exactly
but warming slowly

on which red blossoms
swathed in tulle
assert themselves.
Iron just poured

wreathed in smoke
cooling in the mold.
A wound whispering
through gauze.

Nipple stiffening under
silk. Only the next
world on its way.

Saint Onion

lives mostly in
the dark, head down
in a socket of loam,

on bottom shelves,
in drawers, cabinets,
under sinks, hung in
bags in pantries.

Patron of tissue
paper, bad breath,
dirt. Details

of his martyrdom
are unclear, but you
know the scent of
his auto-de-fe.

Like us, he grew
around himself, layer
by layer, repeating
every mistake.

He comes wrapped
like a gift. Flayed
in bowls on tables
in dim kitchens, he
glows like luminaria

Any meal with
Saint Onion costs tears,
is bitter to make,
joyous to eat.

Moonrise

Always
surprised again
to see that monstrous
stone floating
in the sky.

The sea's our
only hint, sighing
as it warps, hissing
across the sand,
reaching as far
as it can.

Few know
the calculus that
holds the moon
in its arc and
fewer still—

and maybe only
late in strange rooms
waking alone with that
pale spill across
the sheets—

sense what terrible
weight things bear
and still go on.

If you weren't
there, if we didn't
dance, I'd surely
loop away into
the dark.

A miracle
no less than that
a thing so ruined
can shine.

Oyster

I could fly
with these wings
if I chose.
But where
is there to go?

Find a place
and stay put.
Not like the
feckless back-and-
forthing tide.

Your home
is where you are.
If you have a pain
make room.
What you need
will come.

I've lived
a long time
with a hurt.
Now I sleep
with a moon.

The Heron

down at the pond
has his feet wet—
(what's new?)—hunching
like a dour Narcissus
over his reflection. Yet
he sees through it,
and what he sees
feeds him. That spear
between his eyes
insures it. Such
patience—one jab,
one fish.

And stroll is a
considered affair
…like a philosopher
weighing a proposition.
One foot lifted, placed,
the next…

And when he leaves,
it's a surprise. As if
Lincoln's memorial,
Grant's tomb, chose
to lift and imitate
a cloud. A dignified—
a profound event.

With huge, deep strokes
he circles the pond.
Rising…rising…

There Is a River Under the Lake

Years ago
the dam held
up a hand like
a traffic cop
and would not
be disobeyed.

For 100 miles
upstream, seeps
from sloughs,
runnels, creeks,
1000 springs—
all came—
inventing a way.

Every fallen
leaf had the
map—the veins
joining and
joining.

Except for the
trickle staining
the spillway,
all that braided
water slack now,
flat—an Etch-a-
Sketch for the
catspaw breeze.

All night, the vain
moon's mirror.
The wheeling
stars—too
remote to care.

Shores as wide
as the drive
from home
to the office
and back—deep
as a day's worth
of troubles.

Fisherman,
far out under
your wide hat,
cast a line.

Catch the magic
fish. Whisper
the question.
Ask it the way.

Sunset

All the west's awash
with leaving light—
yellows, greens fading
glance by glance and

wisping away one gray
smudge. Leftover smoke … last
scrap something smoldering
somewhere since noon.

Only the latest ending. Vast,
operatic, silent. That mute
orchestra crescendoing
in the pit. Your ticket's
one glance up.

It's likely you'll survive this loss.
This one and the next.
No need to say goodbye.
This one's for practice.

New Moon

Tonight's new moon's an
amber boat above the tree
line's shadowy reef—a skiff,
a delicate shell the old song
says can carry two.

Makes me think of Tristan
and Isolde tossed by
more than the Irish Sea.
Two kids about to fall
into each other—King Mark
be damned.

Could be our kids.
We're old enough to know
what's in the bottle the old
nurse tips into the goblet
(with its silver crescent
chased above a silver sea).

Maybe you're watching
that sliver in the sky.
Maybe you're sailing with it.
Maybe you've sipped
the eldritch brew I've sipped.

Cedar Waxwings

I never see them lush days
when summer can't think anything
but green—only in early spring, the day
after the day the sun almost warms
the still air

Little grayish birds with
a sunrise blush on the breast,
sharp peaked cap, stylish black mask
like revelers at a Venetian ball,
tail-tip dipped in yellow, a dab
of red on the wing.

Puff ball piranhas who, when they find it,
will strip a berry bush to stick.

I hear them first and have to look hard
before they dip to another tree.

This is how we've lived for 100,000 years.
How we still live: family, lovers, friends—
a little band. Everything we've thought
and felt, everything we've said—

…a high, thin piping…
…compact flocks…, the guidebooks say,
…irregular in their wanderings…

For the Birds

out there, singing up the dawn,
going at it like a section gang
laying track. Songs—they tell us—
for mating, for boundaries, meaning
I love you. Here I am.

Shouldn't they be gone—
those tiny compass needles
in their heads pointing south
to fatter feeders, warmer breezes,
Spanish moss? The geese

are—high overhead on their way
like a drill team or a marching band
struggling to get that single
letter right. But the small ones,

they still sing as if they hadn't noticed
dogwoods rusting or frost like powdered
sugar dusting the morning grass.

It won't be long until our dawns are
quiet, their songs gone like all those
words we've said so long will be.
I love you. Here I am.

About the Author

Edward Wilson's poems have appeared in *The American Poetry Review, Beloit Poetry Journal, The Georgia Review, The Midwest Quarterly, Poetry (Chicago), The Southern Poetry Review, The South Carolina Review,* and others. His awards include an Individual Artist Fellowship from the state of Georgia, a Bread Loaf Writers' Conference Fellowship and an NEA Fellowship. He lives in Augusta, Georgia.

CPSIA information can be obtained
at www.ICGtesting.com
Printed in the USA
LVHW050740150419
614196LV00018B/685